This Book BELONGS to

_____

Thanks

Thanks to Sha Nazir for liking my idea and not giving up on it, even when it arrived on his desk in the form of lots of scrappy pieces of paper. The Mighty Women of Science Alphabet Book would not exist without Kate Livingston, Fiona Gordon and Kirsty Hunter, and all the lovely scientists who let me interview them for this book.

Thanks to Robbie, and to my logical and biological family, for keeping me fed and sane.

Dedication

This book is for my niece Katie, who is always mighty in my eyes.

The Mighty Women of Science

Art and story:
Clare Forrest

Words:
Fiona Gordon and Kate Livingston

Designed by
Kirsty Hunter & Sha Nazir

Edited by
Jack Lothian & Nicola Love

First printing 2016
Published in Glasgow by (BHP Comics) Black Hearted Press Ltd.

Made in Scotland. Printed in Great Britain by Bell & Bain Ltd, Glasgow

ISBN: 978-1-910775-06-6
A CIP catalogue reference for this book is available from the British Library

Ask your local comic or book shop to stock BHP Comics. Visit BHPcomics.com for more info.

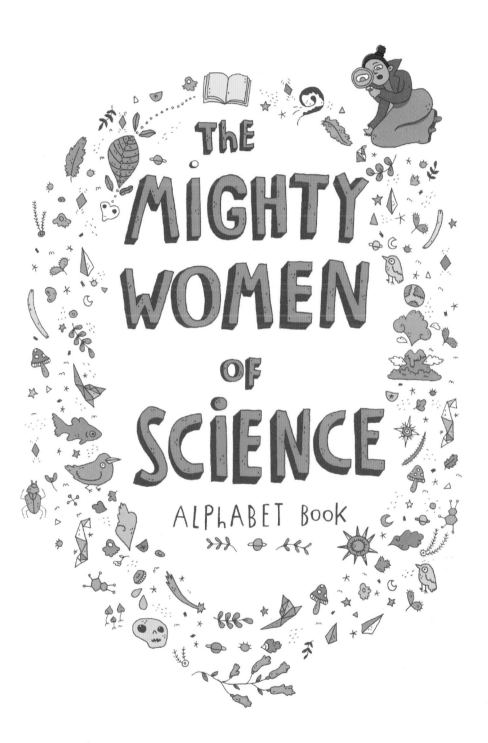

THE MIGHTY WOMEN OF SCIENCE

ALPHABET BOOK

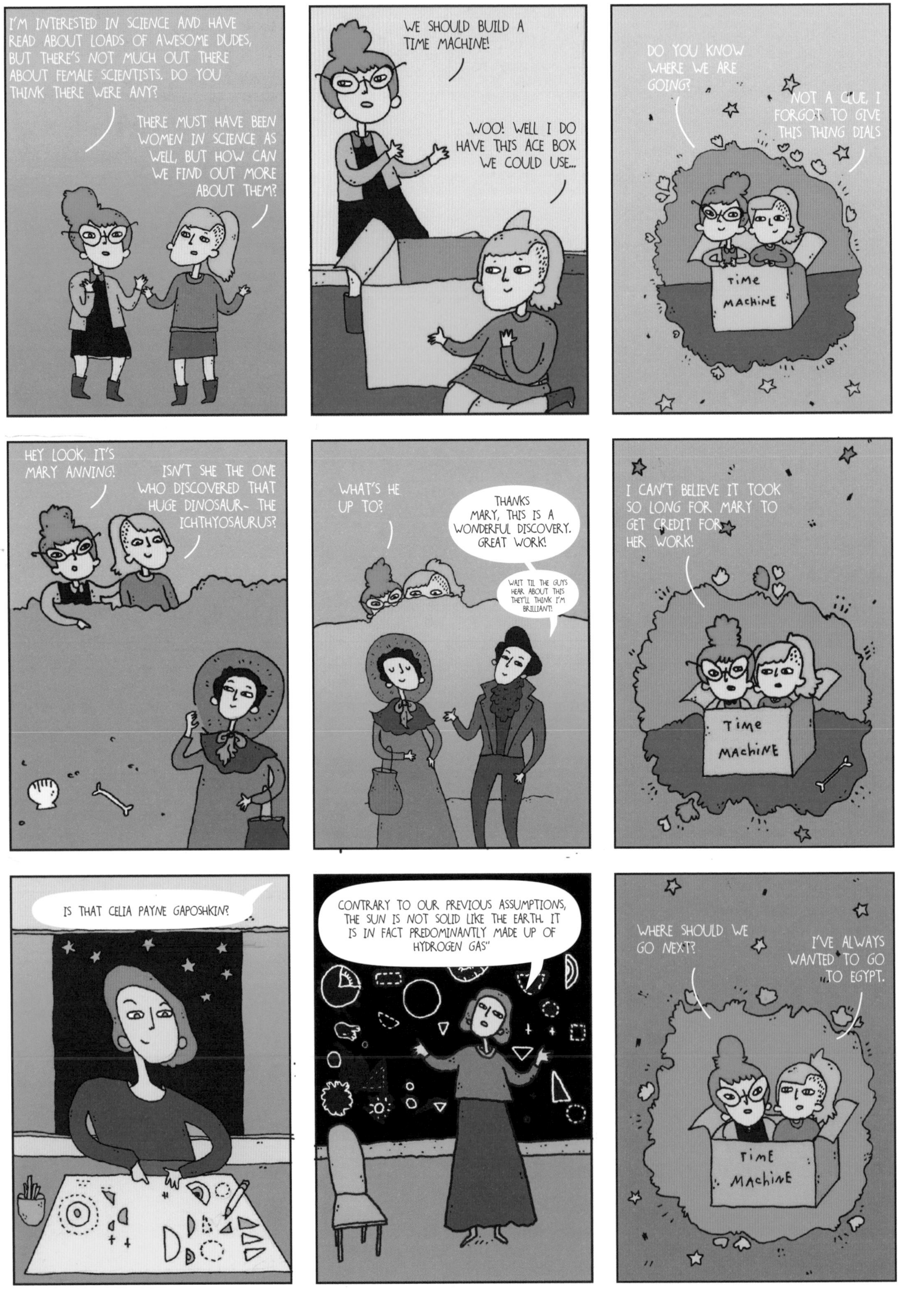
I'M INTERESTED IN SCIENCE AND HAVE READ ABOUT LOADS OF AWESOME DUDES, BUT THERE'S NOT MUCH OUT THERE ABOUT FEMALE SCIENTISTS. DO YOU THINK THERE WERE ANY?
THERE MUST HAVE BEEN WOMEN IN SCIENCE AS WELL, BUT HOW CAN WE FIND OUT MORE ABOUT THEM?
WE SHOULD BUILD A TIME MACHINE!
WOO! WELL I DO HAVE THIS ACE BOX WE COULD USE...
DO YOU KNOW WHERE WE ARE GOING?
NOT A CLUE, I FORGOT TO GIVE THIS THING DIALS
TIME MACHINE
HEY LOOK, IT'S MARY ANNING!
ISN'T SHE THE ONE WHO DISCOVERED THAT HUGE DINOSAUR- THE ICHTHYOSAURUS?
WHAT'S HE UP TO?
THANKS MARY, THIS IS A WONDERFUL DISCOVERY. GREAT WORK!
WAIT TIL THE GUYS HEAR ABOUT THIS THEY'LL THINK I'M BRILLIANT!
I CAN'T BELIEVE IT TOOK SO LONG FOR MARY TO GET CREDIT FOR HER WORK!
TIME MACHINE
IS THAT CELIA PAYNE GAPOSHKIN?
CONTRARY TO OUR PREVIOUS ASSUMPTIONS, THE SUN IS NOT SOLID LIKE THE EARTH. IT IS IN FACT PREDOMINANTLY MADE UP OF HYDROGEN GAS"
WHERE SHOULD WE GO NEXT?
I'VE ALWAYS WANTED TO GO TO EGYPT.
TIME MACHINE

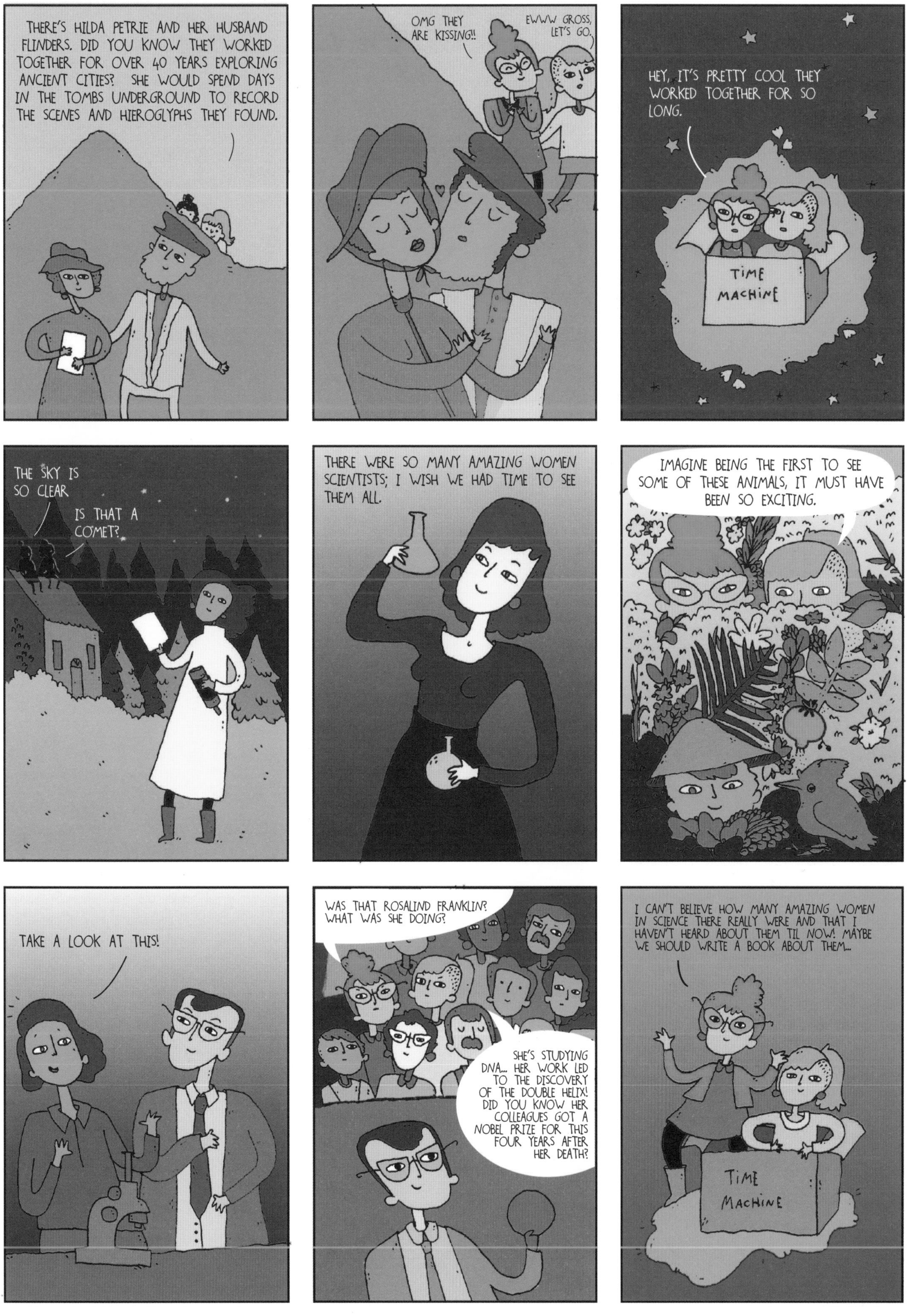
THERE'S HILDA PETRIE AND HER HUSBAND FLINDERS. DID YOU KNOW THEY WORKED TOGETHER FOR OVER 40 YEARS EXPLORING ANCIENT CITIES? SHE WOULD SPEND DAYS IN THE TOMBS UNDERGROUND TO RECORD THE SCENES AND HIEROGLYPHS THEY FOUND.
OMG THEY ARE KISSING!!
EWWW GROSS, LET'S GO.
HEY, IT'S PRETTY COOL THEY WORKED TOGETHER FOR SO LONG.
TIME MACHINE
THE SKY IS SO CLEAR
IS THAT A COMET?
THERE WERE SO MANY AMAZING WOMEN SCIENTISTS; I WISH WE HAD TIME TO SEE THEM ALL.
IMAGINE BEING THE FIRST TO SEE SOME OF THESE ANIMALS, IT MUST HAVE BEEN SO EXCITING.
TAKE A LOOK AT THIS!
WAS THAT ROSALIND FRANKLIN? WHAT WAS SHE DOING?
SHE'S STUDYING DNA... HER WORK LED TO THE DISCOVERY OF THE DOUBLE HELIX! DID YOU KNOW HER COLLEAGUES GOT A NOBEL PRIZE FOR THIS FOUR YEARS AFTER HER DEATH?
I CAN'T BELIEVE HOW MANY AMAZING WOMEN IN SCIENCE THERE REALLY WERE AND THAT I HAVEN'T HEARD ABOUT THEM TIL NOW! MAYBE WE SHOULD WRITE A BOOK ABOUT THEM...
TIME MACHINE

Follow us on a jouney of discovery...

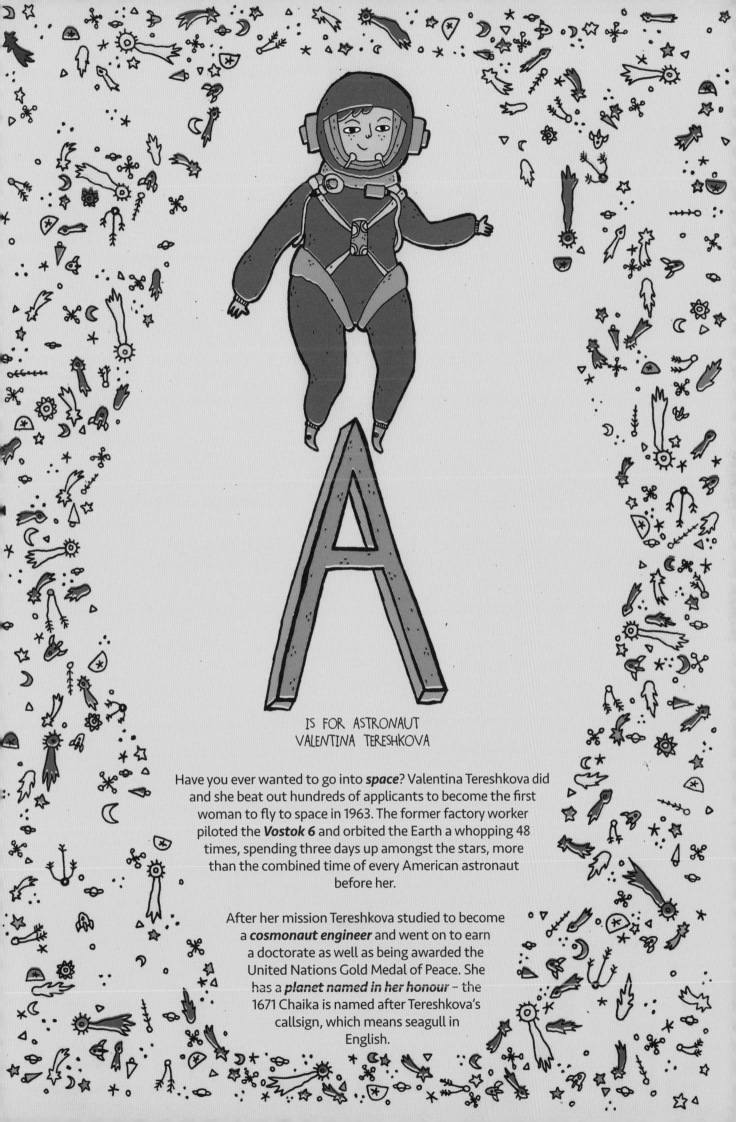

IS FOR ASTRONAUT
VALENTINA TERESHKOVA

Have you ever wanted to go into *space*? Valentina Tereshkova did and she beat out hundreds of applicants to become the first woman to fly to space in 1963. The former factory worker piloted the *Vostok 6* and orbited the Earth a whopping 48 times, spending three days up amongst the stars, more than the combined time of every American astronaut before her.

After her mission Tereshkova studied to become a *cosmonaut engineer* and went on to earn a doctorate as well as being awarded the United Nations Gold Medal of Peace. She has a *planet named in her honour* – the 1671 Chaika is named after Tereshkova's callsign, which means seagull in English.

B

IS FOR BOTANY
JEANNE BARET

Women were **forbidden** on French ships so **botanist** Baret disguised herself as a man, enlisting under the name Jean Baret, so she could embark on her country's first voyage all the way round the world in 1766.

During the trip she collected over **6000 specimens** and helped classify 100s of **plants**, working as an assistant to the famous naturalist Philibert Commerson. While over 70 species of plant are named after Commerson, just one is named after Baret herself: a nightshade called *Solanum Baretiae*, christened almost 250 years after the plant hunter's famous expedition.

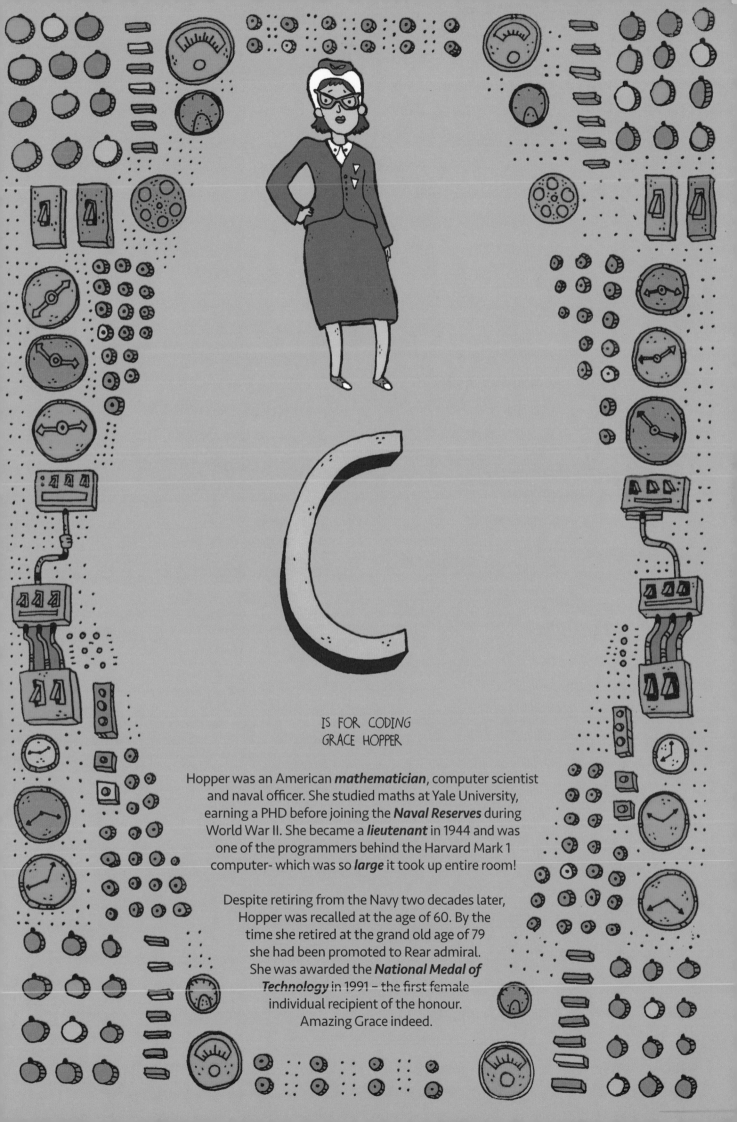

IS FOR CODING
GRACE HOPPER

Hopper was an American **mathematician**, computer scientist and naval officer. She studied maths at Yale University, earning a PHD before joining the **Naval Reserves** during World War II. She became a **lieutenant** in 1944 and was one of the programmers behind the Harvard Mark 1 computer- which was so **large** it took up entire room!

Despite retiring from the Navy two decades later, Hopper was recalled at the age of 60. By the time she retired at the grand old age of 79 she had been promoted to Rear admiral. She was awarded the **National Medal of Technology** in 1991 – the first female individual recipient of the honour. Amazing Grace indeed.

EVA LUCKHIRAM

HELLO! I'M EVA. I'M A PROGRAMMER, DEVELOPER AND DESIGNER OF WEB AND MOBILE APPS. MOST OF MY DAY IS SPENT WRITING CODE IN A VARIETY OF COMPUTER LANGUAGES.

I ALSO DISCUSS WITH WITH MY TEAM THE BEST WAY TO SOLVE PROBLEMS AND CREATE SOFTWARE FOR OUR CLIENTS.

CODING HAD NEVER REALLY BEEN SOMETHING I'D CONSIDERED AS A CAREER.

WHEN I FIRST WENT TO UNI I STUDIED PRODUCT DESIGN BUT I SOON REALISED THAT DEVELOPING MY DIGITAL SKILLS WOULD OPEN UP SOME GREAT OPPORTUNITIES.

BEING A DEVELOPER MEANS THAT I GET TO THINK BOTH CREATIVELY AND LOGICALLY. I LOVE BEING PART OF THE DESIGN PROCESS, THEN PUTING ON MY CODING HAT AND BRINGING THESE DESIGNS TO LIFE.

THE WORLD OF CODE IS CONSTANTLY REWARDING AND FULL OF PERSONAL CAREER HIGHLIGHTS.

SOMETIMES SOMETHING AS SIMPLE AS WRITING A PIECE OF CODE AND GETTING IT TO RUN CAN MAKE YOUR DAY

I LOVE BEING PART OF A TEAM THAT IS RECOGNISED BY OUR PEERS. I HAVE NEVER FELT OUT OF PLACE BEING THE ONLY FEMALE IN THE WORKPLACE.

AS A SOCIETY WE HAVE THIS IMAGE OF CODERS BEING GEEKY AND INTROVERTED AND MALE. I THINK IT IS SO IMPORTANT TO ENCOURAGE MORE WOMEN TO BECOME DEVELOPERS.

I FEEL EMPOWERED TO BE A WOMAN IN THIS INDUSTRY, WHERE TECHNOLOGY IS CONSTANTLY CHANGING AND EACH DAY BRINGS NEW AND EXCITING PROBLEMS TO BE SOLVED.

D

IS FOR DNA
ROSALIND FRANKLIN

English **biophysicist** Franklin is best known for her pioneering work, which led to the discovery of the **DNA double helix**.

First published in 1953, her work is considered to be one of the **most important scientific discoveries** of the 20th century and even won a **Nobel Prize** in 1962. Though Franklin herself was not nominated for the prize – she passed away four years earlier meaning her contribution was not officially recognised – her work is now **globally renowned**.

IS FOR EGYPTOLOGIST
HILDA PETRIE

Arriving in Egypt in 1896, Hilda Petrie spent 45 years digging up and recording **archaeological sites** there and in Palestine. Working alongside her husband, Petrie explored difficult and dangerous conditions; she once spent days lying on the ground recording over **20,000 hieroglyphs** in an underground tomb!

Petrie also worked at the **British School of Archaeology in Egypt**, which her husband founded in 1905. She raised funds which supported the school and allowed her and her husband to continue their missions for years to come.

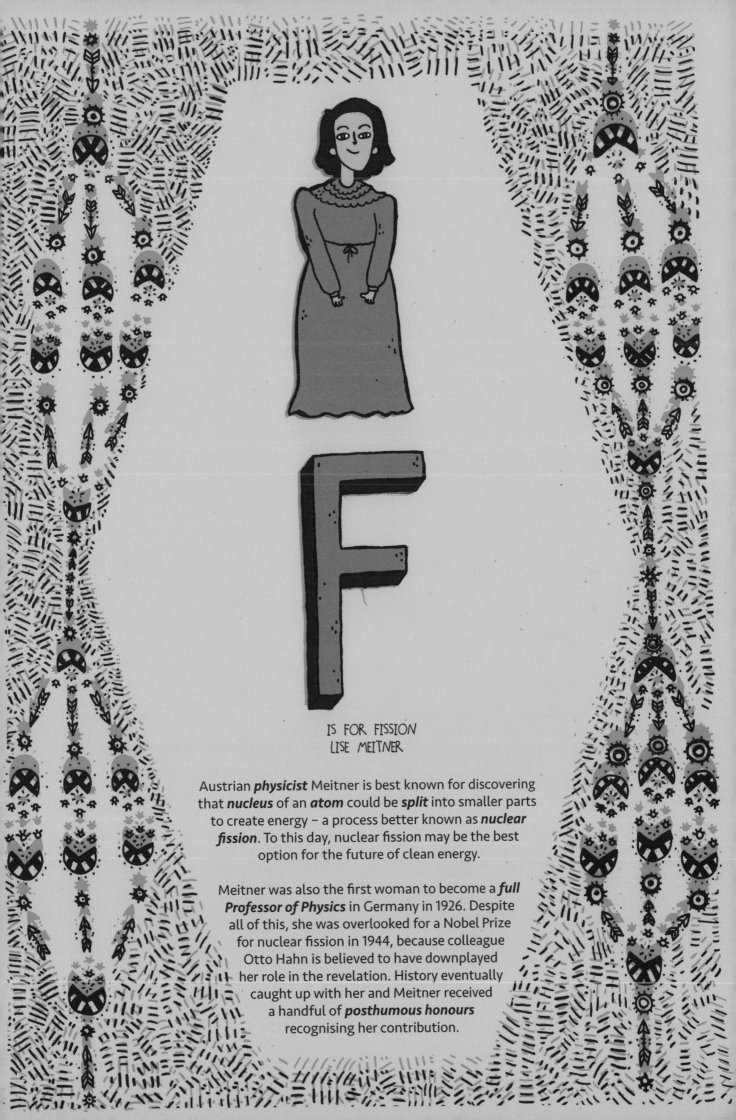

F

IS FOR FISSION
LISE MEITNER

Austrian **physicist** Meitner is best known for discovering that **nucleus** of an **atom** could be **split** into smaller parts to create energy – a process better known as **nuclear fission**. To this day, nuclear fission may be the best option for the future of clean energy.

Meitner was also the first woman to become a **full Professor of Physics** in Germany in 1926. Despite all of this, she was overlooked for a Nobel Prize for nuclear fission in 1944, because colleague Otto Hahn is believed to have downplayed her role in the revelation. History eventually caught up with her and Meitner received a handful of **posthumous honours** recognising her contribution.

G

IS FOR GEOLOGY
MARIE THARP

Do you ever wonder what lies under the sea? Marie Tharp did and this **American geologist** and **oceanographic cartographer** created the first true map of the entire ocean floor. As women were restricted from travelling on research ships she had to create the map using data that her collaborator Bruce Heezen collected at sea.

The map, published in 1977, was **hugely significant**, causing a major shift in scientific thinking towards **plate tectonics**: the theory that the shell of the Earth is covered in plates that shift and move.

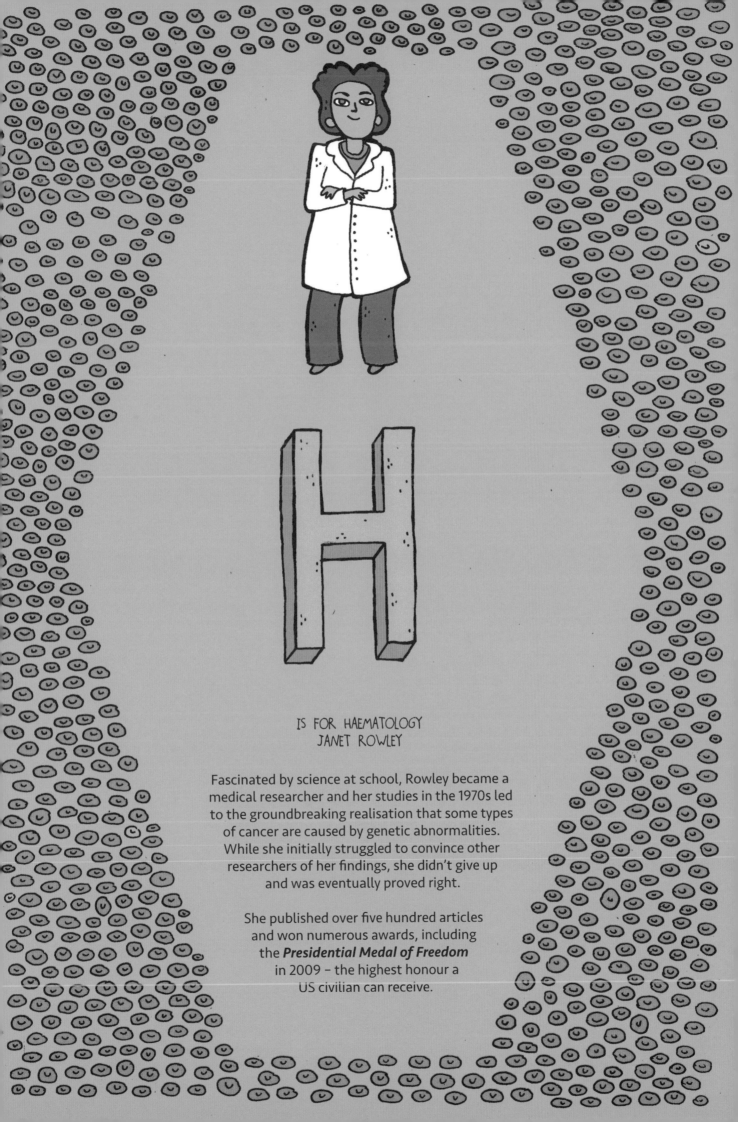

H

IS FOR HAEMATOLOGY
JANET ROWLEY

Fascinated by science at school, Rowley became a
medical researcher and her studies in the 1970s led
to the groundbreaking realisation that some types
of cancer are caused by genetic abnormalities.
While she initially struggled to convince other
researchers of her findings, she didn't give up
and was eventually proved right.

She published over five hundred articles
and won numerous awards, including
the *Presidential Medal of Freedom*
in 2009 – the highest honour a
US civilian can receive.

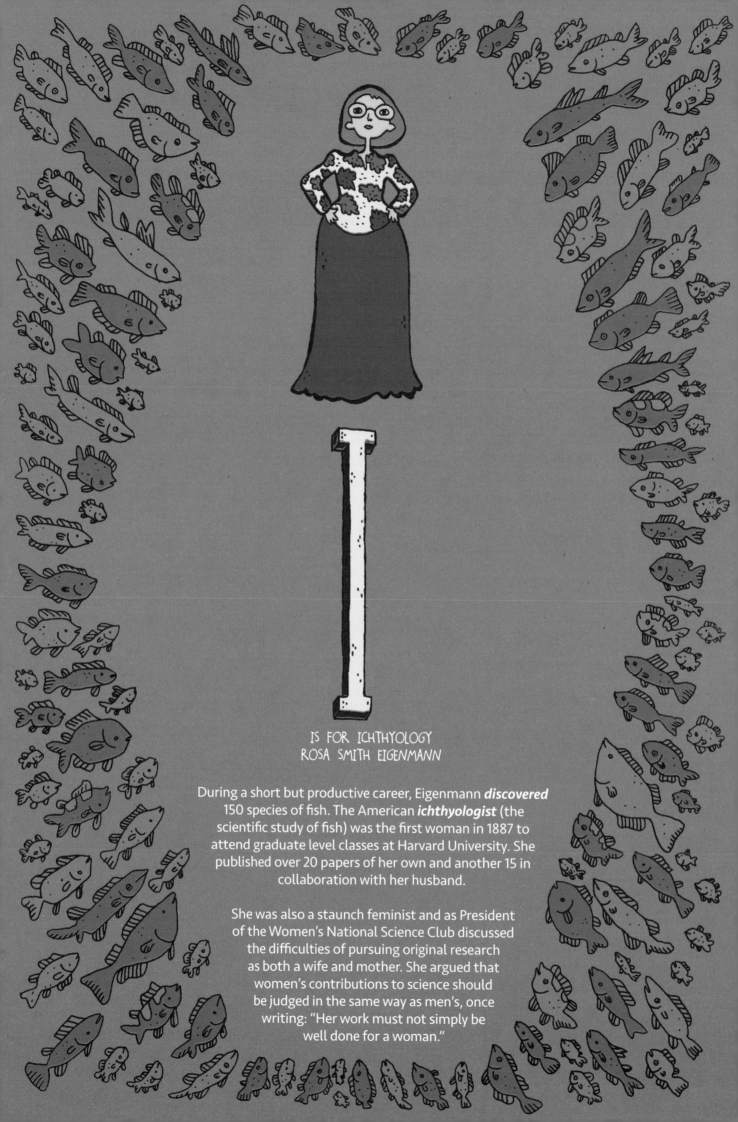

I

IS FOR ICHTHYOLOGY
ROSA SMITH EIGENMANN

During a short but productive career, Eigenmann **discovered** 150 species of fish. The American ***ichthyologist*** (the scientific study of fish) was the first woman in 1887 to attend graduate level classes at Harvard University. She published over 20 papers of her own and another 15 in collaboration with her husband.

She was also a staunch feminist and as President of the Women's National Science Club discussed the difficulties of pursuing original research as both a wife and mother. She argued that women's contributions to science should be judged in the same way as men's, once writing: "Her work must not simply be well done for a woman."

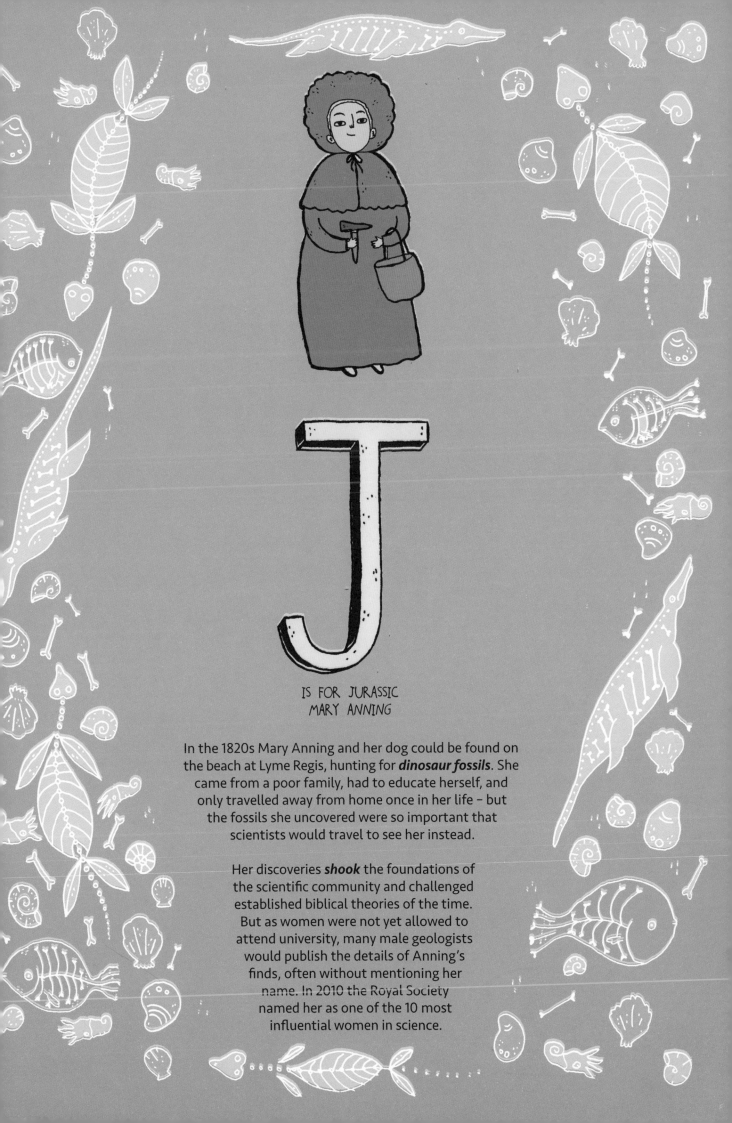

J

IS FOR JURASSIC
MARY ANNING

In the 1820s Mary Anning and her dog could be found on the beach at Lyme Regis, hunting for *dinosaur fossils*. She came from a poor family, had to educate herself, and only travelled away from home once in her life – but the fossils she uncovered were so important that scientists would travel to see her instead.

Her discoveries *shook* the foundations of the scientific community and challenged established biblical theories of the time. But as women were not yet allowed to attend university, many male geologists would publish the details of Anning's finds, often without mentioning her name. In 2010 the Royal Society named her as one of the 10 most influential women in science.

K

IS FOR KINETICS
EMILIE DU CHATELET

In 18th-century France women were not expected to become **mathematicians** or **physicists** but this didn't stop Châtelet from being both- and one of the most influential figures of the century.

Her studies set the ground work for the modern concept of **energy**, the discovery of photography and infrared radiation. Her work on energy and velocity inspired **Einstein's** famous equation of $E = mc^2$ – over 150 years after her death!

IS FOR LICHEN
CLARA EATON CUMMINGS

Botanist Cummings studied *cryptogamic plants* – ones
that reproduce with spores – categorising hundreds
of Lichen specimens over the years. After becoming
an *associate professor* at Wellesley College, she
travelled to Europe in 1886 to study some of the
great botanists.

In 1904 she published a catalogue of over
200 species of Lichens collected during
an Alaskan expedition, including two
which had never been discovered
before! She was also named
president of the Society of Plant
Morphology and Physiology in
the same year.

M

IS FOR MICROBIOLOGY
ESTHER LEDERBERG

This American *microbiologist* is widely recognised as pioneer of *bacterial genetics*, yet it was her husband who got all the credit for the joint work they did, including a Nobel prize – an award he admitted later should have been shared – although he forgot to thank her in his acceptance speech!

Her findings in the 1950s and 60s were *crucial* to advancing the understanding of DNA viruses like E. coli and tumours. Even so, she had to fight to be appointed a professor at Stanford University due to being a woman. Despite her struggles to be recognised, her discoveries changed the face of molecular biology as we know it.

N

IS FOR NEBULAE
CAROLINE HERSCHEL

German-born Herschel was an *astronomer* and the first woman to be paid for her contribution to science. She was also one of the first female members of the *Royal Astronomical Society*.

In 1783 she discovered an open cluster of stars, now known as NGC 2630. She went on to uncover 14 new *nebulae* and, just three years later, became the first women to discover a *comet*. Herschel discovered eight new comets in total, including the periodic comet Herschel-Rigollet which we'll see again in 2092!

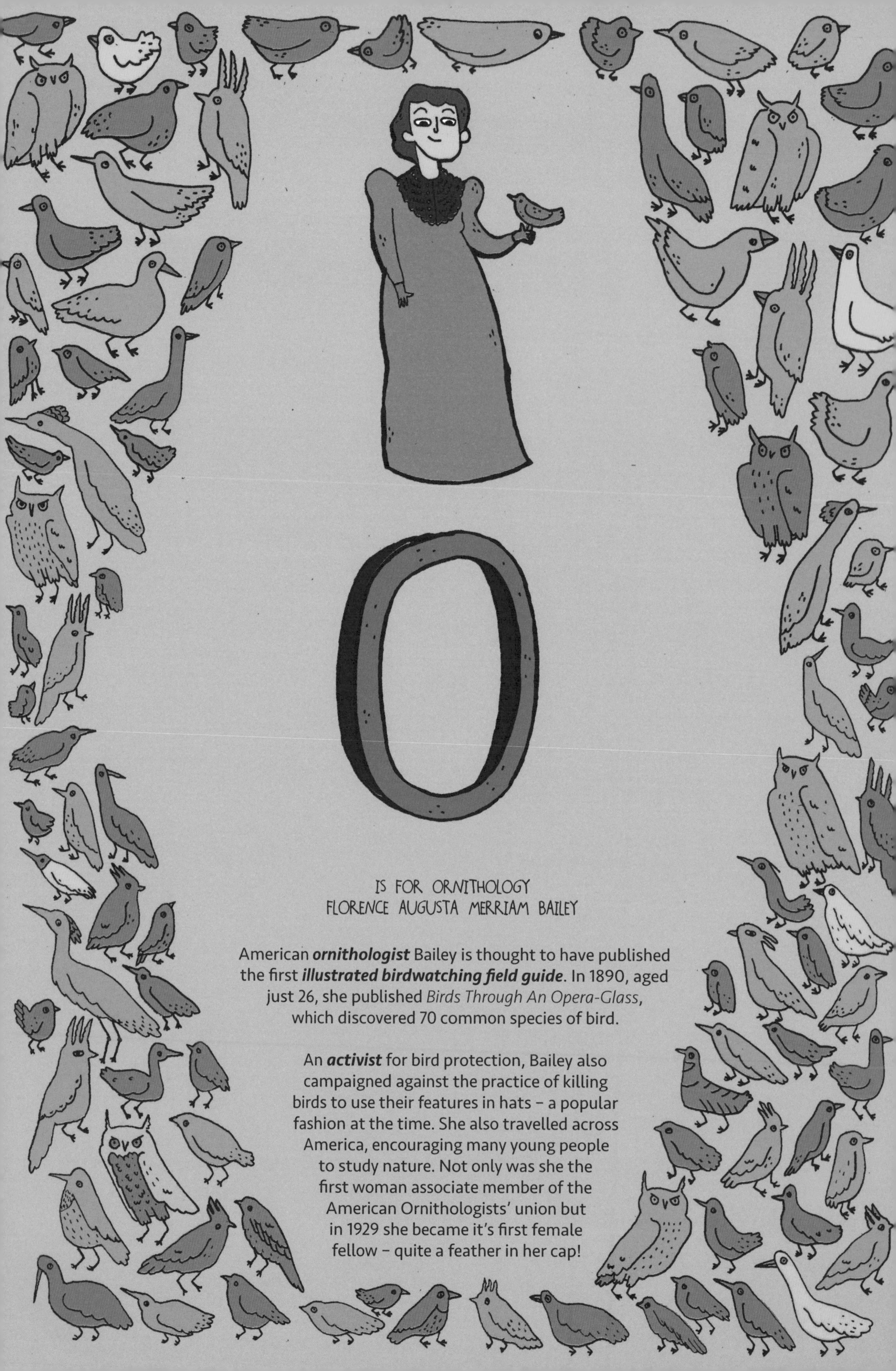
O

IS FOR ORNITHOLOGY
FLORENCE AUGUSTA MERRIAM BAILEY

American ***ornithologist*** Bailey is thought to have published the first ***illustrated birdwatching field guide***. In 1890, aged just 26, she published *Birds Through An Opera-Glass*, which discovered 70 common species of bird.

An ***activist*** for bird protection, Bailey also campaigned against the practice of killing birds to use their features in hats – a popular fashion at the time. She also travelled across America, encouraging many young people to study nature. Not only was she the first woman associate member of the American Ornithologists' union but in 1929 she became it's first female fellow – quite a feather in her cap!

P

IS FOR PLANETS
SARA SEAGER

For centuries humankind has wondered if there are other *planets* that we can live on – or other planets that have life of their own! Sara Seager has made it one of her goals to try and find the answer to that.

This *planetary scientist and astronomer* has won numerous awards (including the prestigious MacArthur Fellowship or "Genius Grant") and is best known for her work on planets outside our solar system – *expolanets* – and their atmospheres, studying them to see which could sustain life. One day we might live amongst the stars – and we'll have Seager to thank for getting us on our way!

SARA SEAGER

HI I'M SARA SEAGER. I'M A PLANETARY SCIENTIST. THIS MEANS I STUDY PLANETS FROM OUR SOLAR SYSTEM AND BEYOND.

I SPEND A LOT OF TIME DEVELOPING DIFFERENT WAYS TO SEARCH FOR PLANETS OUTSIDE OF OUR SOLAR SYSTEM THAT ARE SIMILAR TO EARTH AND I TEACH CLASSES ON PLANETARY AND CLIMATE SCIENCES, TOO.

IT WAS DURING MY TIME AT UNIVERSITY THAT EXOPLANETS WERE FIRST DISCOVERED. I JUMPED AT THE CHANCE TO STUDY THEM!

AN EXOPLANET IS DEFINED AS ANY PLANET THAT ORBITS A STAR OTHER THAN THE SUN. EVERY STAR IN THE SKY IS A SUN, AND EVERY SUN THEORETICALLY HAS ITS OWN SET OF EXOPLANETS.

I AM PARTICULARLY INTERESTED IN PLANETS THAT ORBIT WITHIN THE 'GOLDILOCKS ZONE' OF A STAR...

...WHERE THE TEMPERATURE IS NEITHER TOO HOT OR TOO COLD, AND THE PLANET HAS THE MOST POTENTIAL FOR HARBOURING LIFE.

OUR RESEARCH INTO EXO PLANETS CAN GIVE US A GLIMPSE INTO OUR PAST, AS WELL AS OUR FUTURE, AND HELP US BUILD UP A PICTURE OF OUR OWN SOLAR SYSTEM.

HOW DID OUR SOLAR SYSTEM AND OUR EARTH FORM AND EVOLVE?

WHO OR WHAT IS OUT THERE?

WHAT KINDS OF WORLDS EXIST IN THE VASTNESS OF SPACE?

THE MOST COMMON TYPE OF PLANET IS 2/3 TIMES THE SIZE OF THE EARTH, WHICH HAS NO SOLAR SYSTEM COUNTERPART.

THIS HAS SENT MANY PLANETARY THEORISTS BACK TO THE DRAWING BOARD.

IN THE 1990S A COMMON THEORY WAS THAT BASIC PRINCIPLES OF PHYSICS AND CHEMISTRY ACCOUNTED FOR EVERY MAJOR FEATURE OF THE SOLAR SYSTEM ~ SUCH AS THE ORBITING OF THE PLANETS, THEIR SIZE AND COMPOSITION.

IT WAS THOUGHT THAT THESE PRINCIPLES WOULD APPLY TO THE REST OF THE UNIVERSE, TOO. HOWEVER, WHEN PLANETS WERE DISCOVERED THAT DIDN'T LOOK OR BEHAVE ANYTHING LIKE THOSE IN OUR SOLAR SYSTEM IT WAS CLEAR THAT THE SAME RULES DIDN'T APPLY AFTER ALL.

TO LEARN MORE ABOUT EXOPLANETS THERE ARE A NUMBER OF WAYS TO RESEARCH THEM. WE USE TELESCOPES ON THE GROUND AND IN SPACE.

MY OWN RESEARCH INVOLVES TWO MAIN METHODS OF STUDY. BOTH THESE METHODS ALLOW ME TO EXAMINE THE ATMOSPHERE AROUND AN EXOPLANET SO THAT I CAN DETECT TINY CHEMICAL SIGNATURES WHICH CAN INDICATE LIFE.

ONE METHOD I USE IS THE TRANSIT METHOD.

IF A PLANET GOES IN FRONT OF THE STAR DURING ITS ORBIT, THEN THE STARLIGHT DIMS BY A TINY AMOUNT.

ASTRONOMERS USE VERY POWERFUL DETECTORS ON TELESCOPES TO RECORD THE BRIGHTNESS OF A STAR AND DETECT THIS KIND OF DIMMING. TRANSITS ARE RARE, BECAUSE THE PLANET AND THE STAR MUST BE ALIGNED FOR THE DIMMING TO TAKE PLACE.

THIS MEANS THAT MANY STARS HAVE TO BE MONITORED AT THE SAME TIME. THE KEPLER MISSION ~ A SPACE OBSERVATORY LAUNCHED BY NASA TO SEARCH FOR EARTH-LIKE PLANETS ~ DID JUST THAT, MONITORING 150,000 STARS OVER 4 YEARS.

THE SECOND METHOD I USE IS DIRECT IMAGING, WHICH TAKES A PICTURE OF THE PLANET ITSELF. THE CHALLENGE WITH THIS IS THAT THE HOST STAR IS MUCH BRIGHTER THAN THE PLANET ITSELF, SO IT CAN BE NEARLY IMPOSSIBLE TO SEE THE PLANET.

ASTRONOMERS HAVE FOUND A WAY TO BLOCK OUT THE STAR LIGHT AND SEE THE PLANET DIRECTLY. THIS INVOLVES ADAPTIVE OPTICS, A TECHNOLOGY USED TO REDUCE DISTORTIONS IN LIGHT WAVES, PLACED INSIDE A TELESCOPE.

"WE'RE CURRENTLY WORKING ON 'THE STARSHADE'"

"THIS IS A GIANT LENS THAT WILL FLY IN SPACE TO BLOCK THE LIGHT OF STARS SO THAT WE CAN SEARCH FOR SMALLER PLANETS."

ANOTHER REASON TO STUDY EXOPLANETS IS THAT THINGS WE DEVELOP CAN SOMETIMES BE USED IN UNEXPECTED AND LIFE-ALTERING WAYS.

FOR EXAMPLE, THE LASER HAS MANY USEFUL APPLICATIONS THAT REACH FAR BEYOND ITS ORIGINAL INTENDED USE. IT WAS ORIGINALLY DEVELOPED FOR APPLICATIONS SUCH AS SPECTROMETRY, RADAR AND NUCLEAR FUSION.

TODAY IT IS USED FOR SCANNING BARCODES, SURGERY, CREATING ART AND TECHNOLOGY - AND SCARING CATS.

OTHER THINGS THAT HAVE COME FROM DEVELOPMENTS MADE IN PLANETARY EXPLORATION ARE MEDICAL IMAGING, DNA TESTING, THE INTERNET AND GPS.

http://theinternet.com

IT'S IMPORTANT TO SUPPORT PURE SCIENCE RESEARCH NEEDED TO ENABLE SUCH TECHNOLOGICAL BREAKTHROUGHS. ALTHOUGH THESE CAN BE RARE, THEY INVARIABLY CHANGE OUR WORLD.

I HAVE HAD MANY THINGS IN MY CAREER THAT I CAN BE PROUD OF HOWEVER THERE ARE A FEW HIGHLIGHTS I AM PARTICULARY PROUD OF.

CINEMA
STAR WARS

I CHERISH EACH NEW DAY

AS IF I WERE DISCOVERING THE WORLD FOR THE FIRST TIME.

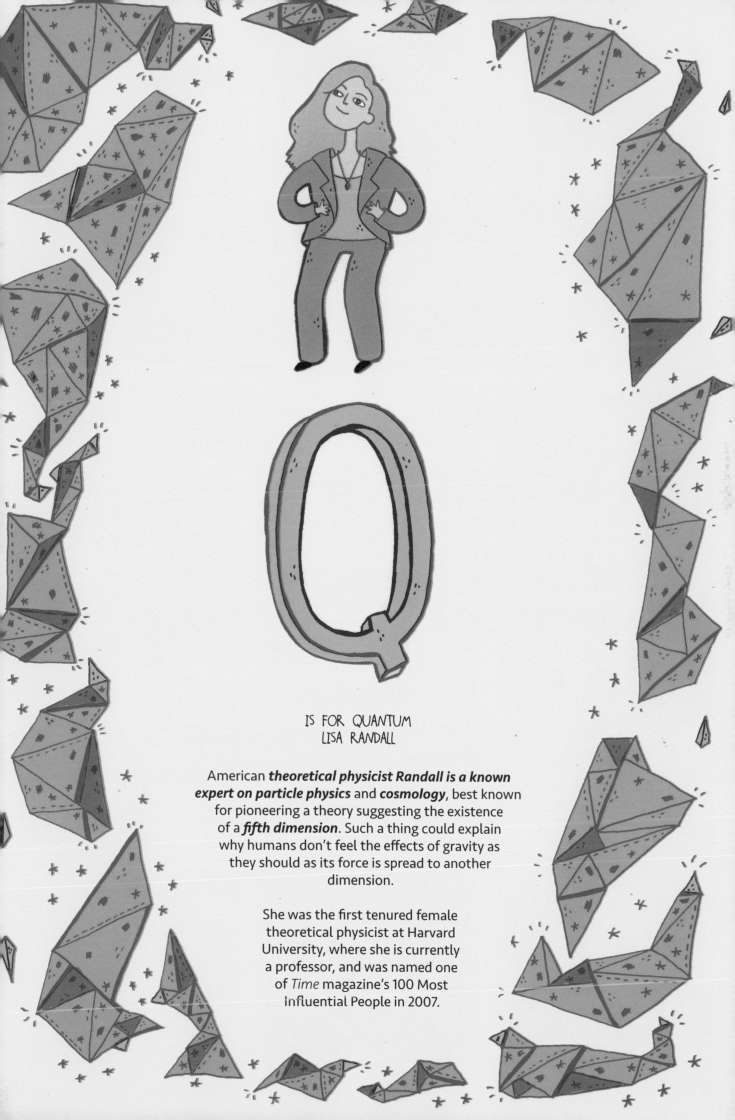

Q

IS FOR QUANTUM
LISA RANDALL

American **theoretical physicist Randall is a known
expert on particle physics** and **cosmology**, best known
for pioneering a theory suggesting the existence
of a **fifth dimension**. Such a thing could explain
why humans don't feel the effects of gravity as
they should as its force is spread to another
dimension.

She was the first tenured female
theoretical physicist at Harvard
University, where she is currently
a professor, and was named one
of *Time* magazine's 100 Most
Influential People in 2007.

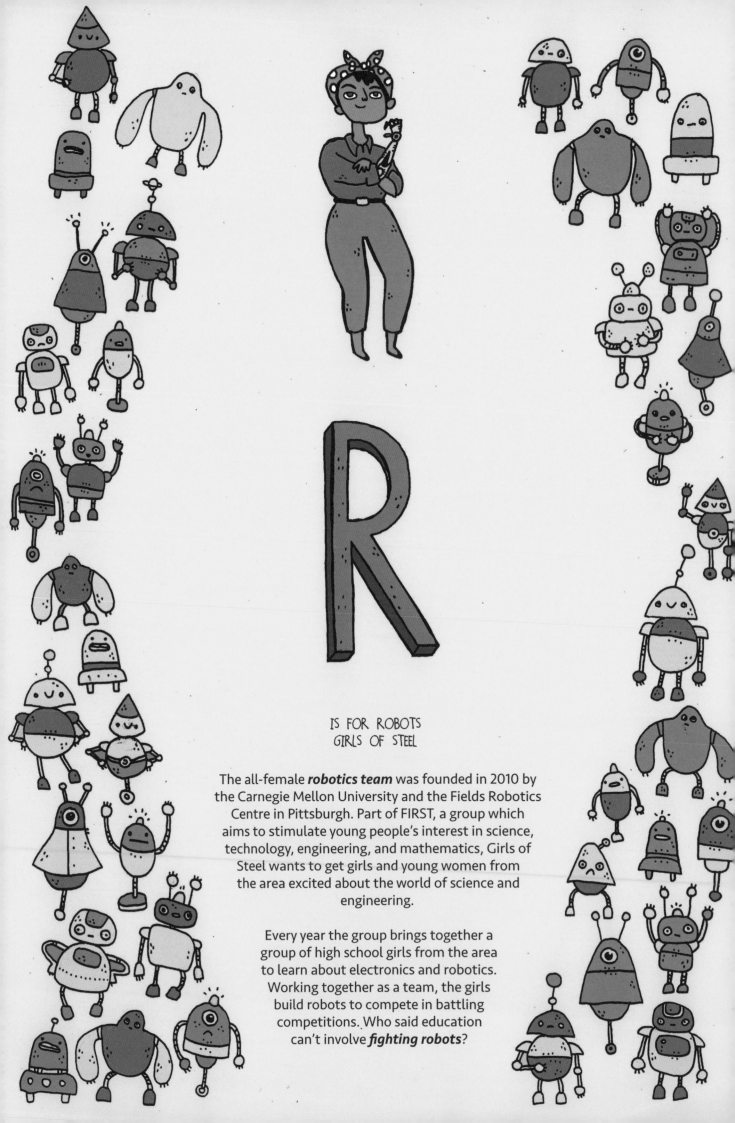

R

IS FOR ROBOTS
GIRLS OF STEEL

The all-female *robotics team* was founded in 2010 by the Carnegie Mellon University and the Fields Robotics Centre in Pittsburgh. Part of FIRST, a group which aims to stimulate young people's interest in science, technology, engineering, and mathematics, Girls of Steel wants to get girls and young women from the area excited about the world of science and engineering.

Every year the group brings together a group of high school girls from the area to learn about electronics and robotics. Working together as a team, the girls build robots to compete in battling competitions. Who said education can't involve *fighting robots*?

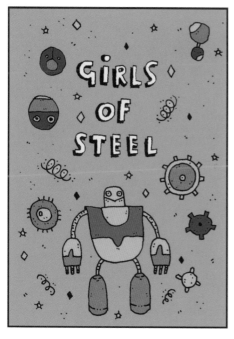

GIRLS OF STEEL IS AN ALL GIRLS ROBOTICS TEAM FOR 8TH-12TH GRADERS IN THE PITTSBURG AREA ~ EVERY YEAR WE WORK TOGETHER TO BUILD ROBOTS TO COMPETE IN ROBOT BATTLING COMPETITIONS.

WE FIRST BEGAN IN 2010 WITH A TEAM MADE UP OF 24 GIRLS FROM 12 DIFFERENT SCHOOLS. WE STARTED OUR 2015-16 SEASON WITH A TEAM OF 76!

OUR NAME, "GIRLS OF STEEL" MESHES PERFECTLY WITH OUR LOGO ~ ROSIE THE RIVETER WITH A ROBOTIC ARM. ROSIE IS A REAL SYMBOL OF FEMALE EMPOWERMENT.

"WE CAN DO IT" IS ROSIE'S FAMOUS SAYING. IN A MALE~DOMINATED FIELD, WE BELIEVE THAT IT IS CRUCIAL FOR WOMEN AND GIRLS TO FEEL RESPECTED AS STRONG, HARD WORKERS

THERE'S A REAL LACK OF GIRLS IN THE FIELD OF ROBOTICS AT THE MOMENT, SO WE HOPE THAT GIRLS OF STEEL WILL PAVE THE WAY TO ALLOW THAT TO CHANGE.

FOR EXAMPLE, AT THE U.S DARPA ROBOTICS CHALLENGE ~ FOR ROBOTS THAT CAN DO COMPLEX TASKS IN DANGEROUS ENVIRONMENTS ~ I COULDN'T BELIEVE THAT ON ANY OF THE LARGE TEAMS THERE WASN'T ONE FEMALE.

WOMEN ARE HALF THE POPULATION, SO IT MAKES SENSE TO ME THAT FOR OUR WORLD TO BE THE BEST IT CAN BE WE SHOULD USE THE COLLECTIVE INTELLIGENCE OF ALL OF OUR MINDS ~ NOT JUST THE MALE HALF.

I LOVE BEING PART OF GIRLS OF STEEL. WHEN I'M THERE I FEEL LIKE GENDER ISN'T AN ISSUE. I'M SO INSPIRED BY THE GIRLS AROUND ME AND MY PEERS ON THE TEAM.

IT'S GOOD TO BE ABLE TO RELAX AND GET AS INVOLVED AS I WANT TO, BECAUSE I DON'T THINK THAT WOULD BE AS EASY FOR ME IN A CO-ED TEAM. I GET TO INTERACT WITH SO MANY OTHER PEOPLE TOO.

BEING PART OF THE TEAM HAS HELPED TO BUILD OUR CONFIDENCE AND COMMUNICATION SKILLS. WE HAVE SUCH A GREAT COMMUNITY OF GIRLS WORKING TOGETHER IN A POSITIVE AND SUPPORTIVE ENVIRONMENT TOWARDS A COMMON GOAL.

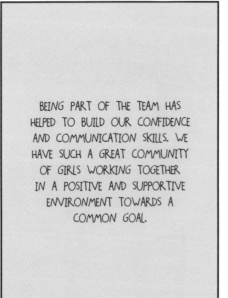

ONE OF THE COMPETITIONS WE ENTER IS THE FIRST ROBOTICS COMPETITION - FRC - WHERE YOUR TEAM HAS 6 WEEKS TO BUILD A GAME-PLAYING ROBOT.

IN 2015 WE WON THE MEDIA AND INNOVATION AWARD AT THE FRC WORLD CHAMPIONSHIPS. WE ALSO WON THE CHAIRMAN'S AWARD AT THE FRC ROBOTICS BUCKEYE REGIONAL.

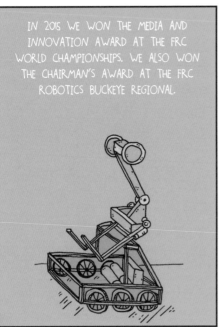

EVERY YEAR WE FACE THE SAME CHALLENGE- HOW DO WE BUILD OUR ROBOT AND MAKE IT THE BEST IT CAN BE IN SUCH A LIMITED TIME?

MY TEAM IS SO INSPIRING. OUR TEAM MENTOR, PATTI ROTE, HELPED TO FOUND THE TEAM AND SHE DOES SO MUCH FOR ALL OF US. SHE REALLY IS AMAZING AND SO IMPORTANT TO US.

SINCE JOINING GIRLS OF STEEL I'VE HAD SO MANY OPPORTUNITIES AND EXPERIENCES THAT I WOULDN'T HAVE HAD OTHERWISE. I'VE MADE LOTS OF FRIENDS AND I TOTALLY LOVED THE EXPERIENCE OF BUILDING A ROBOT TOGETHER.

SO MUCH OF GIRLS OF STEEL IS ABOUT TEAMWORK. NOTHING BEATS THE FEELING OF ALL BEING TOGETHER AND CHEERING ON YOUR ROBOT AT A COMPETITION!

WE HOPE TO GET AS MANY PEOPLE AS POSSIBLE - AND MORE AND MORE GIRLS - INVOLVED IN STEM.

S

IS FOR STELLAR
CELIA PAYNE GAPOSHKIN

Born in England in 1900, this **astronomer** and **astrophysicist** moved to America after gaining a fellowship to study at Harvard College Observatory. In 1925, Payne proposed that **stars** consisted of mostly **hydrogen** and **helium**. At the time this theory was **extremely controversial** as it was believed that stars – including the sun – were made of the same elements as earth.

Astronomer Henry Norris Russell reviewed her dissertation and encouraged Payne not to publish this conclusion. Four years later, following his own research, Russell would publish the discovery himself – with only a **brief acknowledgement** for Payne's work. Thankfully her trailblazing work is now widely recognised and she was an inspiration to many scientists who followed her.

T

IS FOR TYRANNOSAURUS
MARY HIGBY SCHWEITZER

In 2007 this American born **paleontologist** (a scientist who studies fossils) was the first person to find preserved soft tissue from a dinosaur – using a 68 million year old leg bone from a **Tyrannosaurus** skeleton. Using the blood cells and soft tissue remains, she was also able to find evidence that the specimen was a pregnant female.

Schweitzer's work showed molecular similarities between the tyrannosaurus remains and the chicken, providing further evidence of the relationship between **birds** and **dinosaurs**.

U

IS FOR UNIVERSE
HENRIETTA SWAN LEAVITT

Do you know what variable stars are? They're stars that change brightness. Leavitt discovered over 1,200 of them as well a method of measuring and cataloguing the brightness during the 1900s.

The discovery was known as the **period-luminosity relationship** and provided a measurement for astronomers to calculate the distance between the earth and the stars. This changed the picture of our *universe*, and laid the foundations for Edwin Hubble's Nobel Prize-winning theory that the universe is expanding.

She has an asteroid and moon crater named after her – honouring deaf men and women, like herself, who worked as astronomers.

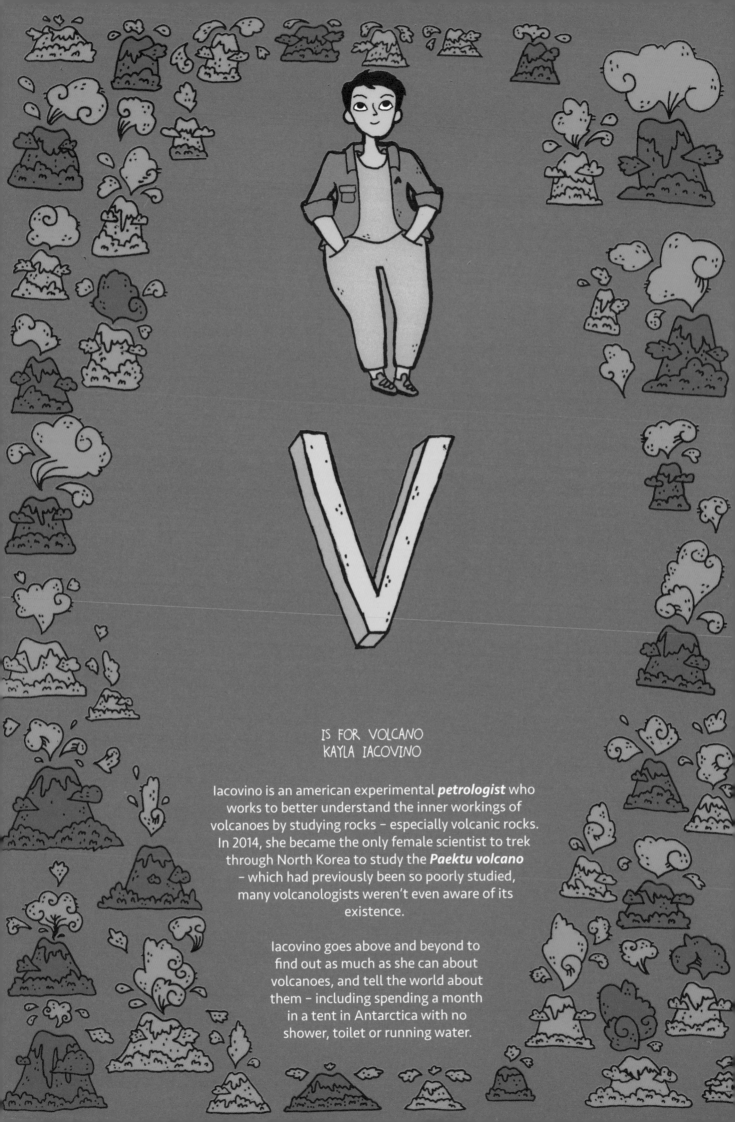

V

IS FOR VOLCANO
KAYLA IACOVINO

Iacovino is an american experimental **petrologist** who works to better understand the inner workings of volcanoes by studying rocks – especially volcanic rocks. In 2014, she became the only female scientist to trek through North Korea to study the **Paektu volcano** – which had previously been so poorly studied, many volcanologists weren't even aware of its existence.

Iacovino goes above and beyond to find out as much as she can about volcanoes, and tell the world about them – including spending a month in a tent in Antarctica with no shower, toilet or running water.

HI! I'M KAYLA. I'M A VOLCANOLOGIST AND EXPERIMENTAL PETROLOGIST.

I STUDY VOLCANOES: HOW THEY WORK, WHAT THEY ARE UP TO UNDERGROUND BEFORE THEY ERUPT.

I ALSO STUDY ROCKS, SPECIFICALLY THE ORIGINS OF VOLCANIC ROCKS.

I WANT TO KNOW EVERYTHING A PIECE OF LAVA OR PUMICE HAS BEEN THROUGH, FROM ITS INCEPTION WITHIN THE EARTH, TO ITS ERUPTION AND COOLING ON THE PLANET'S SURFACE.

I USE HIGH PRESSURE AND HIGH TEMPERATURE EQUIPMENT TO SIMULATE THE INSIDE OF A VOLCANO.

THIS LETS ME TURN BACK THE CLOCK TO SEE WHAT VOLCANIC ROCKS LOOKED LIKE BEFORE THEY ERUPTED.

BY LOOKING AT VARIOUS STAGES OF A ROCK'S DEVELOPMENT, WE CAN FIND OUT ABOUT THE ENVIRONMENT THEY WERE IN WHILE THEY WERE EVOLVING DEEP UNDERGROUND.

I CAN TRACE MY INTEREST IN VOLCANOLOGY BACK TO ONE SINGLE EMAIL. THE SUBJECT LINE READ: "GET PAID TO MELT ROCKS!"

IT WAS A JOB ADVERTISEMENT FOR AN UNDERGRADUATE RESEARCHER IN AN EXPERIMENTAL PETROLOGY LAB. HOW COULD I NOT APPLY?

I DID MY UNDERGRADUATE DEGREE AT ARIZONA STATE UNIVERSITY. ASU IS WHERE I LEARNED TO LOVE ROCKS, VOLCANOES AND WHAT IT MEANS TO BE A SCIENTIST.

AT THE UNIVERSITY OF CAMBRIDGE, DURING MY PHD STUDIES, I WAS SURROUNDED BY SUCH AN INVIGORATING ACADEMIC ENVIRONMENT ALL THE TIME. I MET PEOPLE FROM ALL OVER THE WORLD, AND I GOT TO LIVE ALL OVER EUROPE DURING MY TIME THERE.

I CURRENTLY WORK AT THE US GEOLOGICAL SURVEY IN MENLO PARK, CALIFORNIA. THERE ARE SO MANY GEOLOGISTS HERE THAT IF I HAVE A QUESTION ABOUT PRETTY MUCH ANY ASPECT OF A ROCK OR GEOLOGICAL PROCESS, THERE IS BOUND TO BE SOMEONE WHO IS AN EXPERT ON THAT VERY THING!

THERE ISN'T REALLY 'A TYPICAL WORK DAY' FOR ME. I GET TO DO DIFFERENT THINGS ALL THE TIME. SOME DAYS I SPEND IN THE LAB PERFORMING EXPERIMENTS OR PREPARING ROCK SAMPLES.

OTHER DAYS I SPEND ANALYZING SAMPLES ON A VARIETY OF INCREDIBLY COMPLICATED MACHINES. SOMETIMES I AM STUCK DOING SPREADSHEETS. I ALSO DO A LOT OF EDUCATIONAL OUTREACH ~ I MAKE VIDEOS, WRITE BLOGS OR GO TO SCHOOLS AND FESTIVALS TO DO VOLCANO DEMOS.

BUT BEST OF ALL, SOME TIMES I CAN FIND MYSELF ON THE SIDE OF A VOLCANO IN THE MIDDLE OF THE JUNGLE, ARTIC, DESERT, OR EVEN NORTH KOREA!

I WAS ONCE IN A GROUP THAT WAS THE TARGET OF A KIDNAPPING OF TOURISTS, SCIENTISTS AND GUIDES IN ETHIOPIA. LUCKILY WE WERE BEHIND SCHEDULE BY 24 HOURS, OTHERWISE WE WOULD HAVE BEEN AT THE TOP OF THE VOLCANO AND BEFALLEN THE SAME FATE AS THOSE WHO WERE THERE THAT NIGHT.

GEOLOGY DOES A GOOD JOB EMPOWERING WOMEN AND RECRUITING THEM IN THE FIELD. HOWEVER, BEING A WOMAN IN SCIENCE MEANS YOU ARE GOING TO FACE SOME CHALLENGES. ACADEMICS CAN BE VERY COMPETITIVE, AND I HAVE WORKED WITH MEN WHO WILL NEVER HAVE AS MUCH RESPECT FOR ME AS THEY WOULD HAVE IF I WERE MALE.

LUCKILY, I'VE NOT ENCOUNTERED TOO MANY PEOPLE LIKE THAT.

I HAVE SO MANY THINGS ON MY LIST THAT I WANT TO DO, AND SO MANY VOLCANOES I WANT TO VISIT. I WANT TO ESTABLISH MY OWN LABORATORY THAT STUDIES ALL KINDS OF MAGMATIC ACTIVITY IN THE EARTH'S CRUST AND MANTLE.

MY DREAM IS TO TURN THAT LAB IN TO A PLACE WHERE I CAN HELP LOTS OF UNDERGRADUATE STUDENTS HAVE THE SAME AMAZING EXPERIENCE I HAD DURING MY STUDIES.

THE PEOPLE WHO HAVE INSPIRED ME ARE THE PEOPLE THAT I'VE WORKED WITH ON A DAILY BASIS. THEY ARE THE MOST AMAZING AND INTELLIGENT PEOPLE THAT I'VE EVER MET, AND HAVE ALL SHAPED AND INSPIRED ME. I HOPE THAT ONE DAY I CAN DO THE SAME FOR YOUNGER GENERATIONS.

W

IS FOR WEATHER
JOANNE MALKUS SIMPSON

In 1949, Simpson became the first woman to ever receive a phd in *meteorology*. She was also the first person to develop a scientific model of clouds, revealing that they were what caused the weather – not just a result of it.

Simpson made a number of *groundbreaking discoveries* in the 1950s and 60s, including discovering the driving force behind hurricanes and was named one of the Top Ten Female Role Models by the Ms. Foundation in 1998, by which time she was NASA's *chief scientist* for meteorology.

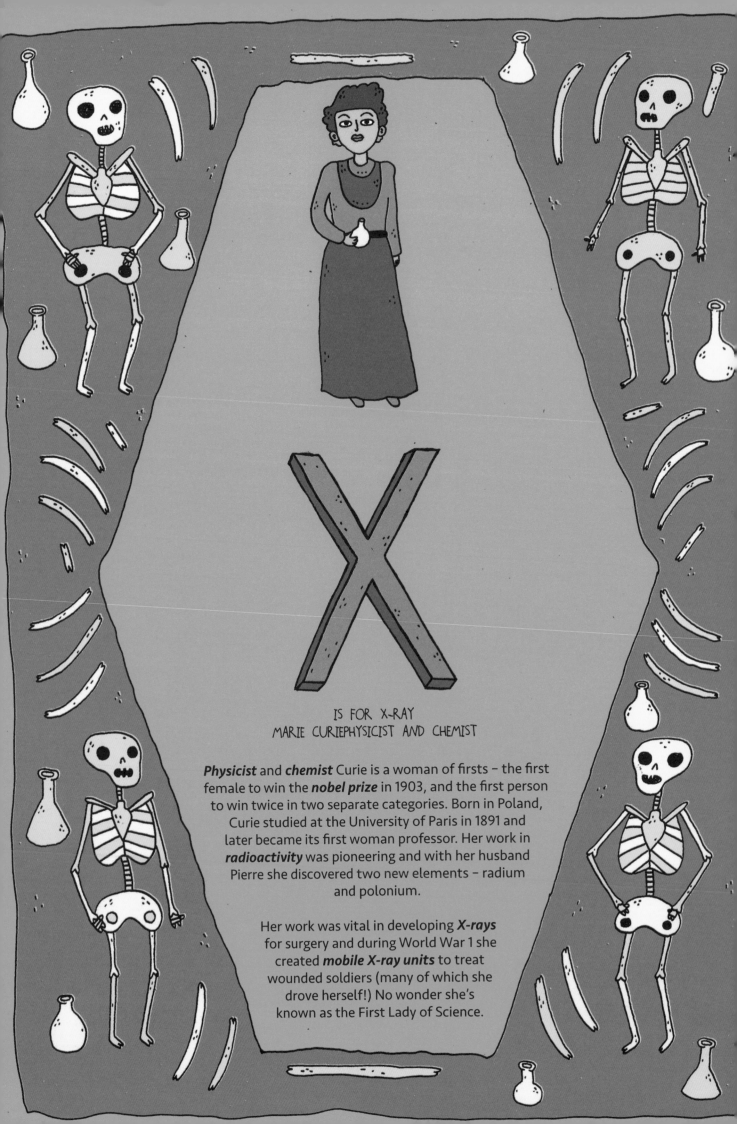

IS FOR X-RAY
MARIE CURIE PHYSICIST AND CHEMIST

Physicist and **chemist** Curie is a woman of firsts – the first female to win the **nobel prize** in 1903, and the first person to win twice in two separate categories. Born in Poland, Curie studied at the University of Paris in 1891 and later became its first woman professor. Her work in **radioactivity** was pioneering and with her husband Pierre she discovered two new elements – radium and polonium.

Her work was vital in developing **X-rays** for surgery and during World War 1 she created **mobile X-ray units** to treat wounded soldiers (many of which she drove herself!) No wonder she's known as the First Lady of Science.

Y

IS FOR Y-CHROMOSOME
NETTIE STEVENS

What causes us to be **born** as either a man or a woman? Until
Nettie Stevens discovered the Y chromosome in 1905 it was
still quite a puzzle. *Geneticist* Stevens started out as a school
teacher – saving money for 15 years until she was finally able
to afford university at the age of 35 in 1896. She received
her PhD in 1903 and two years later she made her great
discovery.

At the time scientists still didn't really know
what caused us to be a man or a woman – the
X chromosome had been found but it wasn't
until Stevens discovered the partnering
Y chromosome that the picture was
complete. Before this it was believed
that the mother or the environment
would determine the sex of a child.

Z

IS FOR ZOOLOGY
BIRUTE GALDIKAS

How would you like to spend thirty years working in the rainforest, dealing with poachers, leeches and deadly insects? That's what the renowned **scientist** and **conservationist** Galdikas did for over three decades, studying **orangutans** in their natural environment as well as working to free captive ones and release them back into the wild.

Galdikas is one of a trio of women who studied **primates** in their natural environment in the 1970s, along with Jane Godall and Dian Fossey. Now a world renowned expert in orangutan behaviour, and a university professor, she spends much of her time campaigning for the preservation of the **rainforest**.

IT'S BEEN A LOT OF FUN RESEARCHING THE GROUNDBREAKING FEMALE SCIENTISTS OF THE PAST, BUT THERE ARE STILL SOME GAPS IN OUR BOOK. DO YOU THINK THINGS ARE DIFFERENT TODAY FOR WOMEN IN SCIENCE?

OOOOHH

WANNA GO VISIT SOME OF THEM?

YES!

TIME MACHINE

THIS IS SARA SEAGER'S 40TH BIRTHDAY! INSTEAD OF ASKING FOR PRESENTS, SHE ASKED GUESTS TO HELP HER FIND ANOTHER EARTH IN HER LIFETIME.

DO YOU THINK WE'LL EVER FIND ANOTHER HABITABLE PLANET? ONE THAT'S JUST LIKE EARTH?

I HOPE SO. MAYBE WE'LL FIND A WAY TO TRAVEL THERE ONE DAY, TOO!

OOPS! WRONG TURN, IS THIS THING SHARK PROOF?

LET'S GET OUT OF HERE!

TIME MACHINE

PHEW!

TIME MACHINE

OH HEY, I THINK THAT'S BIRUTE GALDIKAS!

WHO'S SHE?

TIME MACHINE

SHE WAS KIND OF THE FIRST PERSON TO REALLY STUDY ORANG-UTANS. UNTIL SHE STARTED RESEARCHING THEM THERE WAS VERY LITTLE KNOWN ABOUT THEM AT ALL.

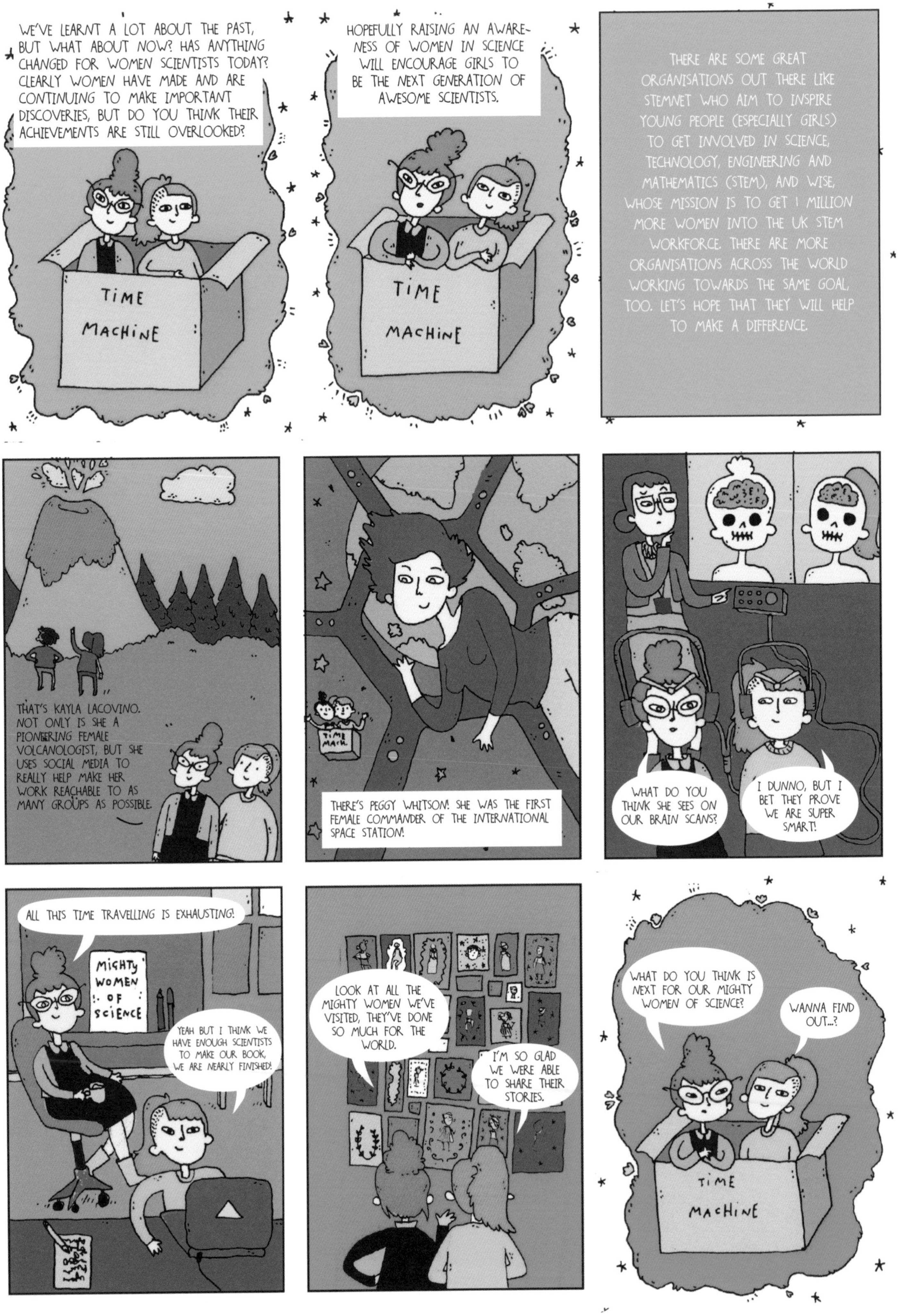
WE'VE LEARNT A LOT ABOUT THE PAST, BUT WHAT ABOUT NOW? HAS ANYTHING CHANGED FOR WOMEN SCIENTISTS TODAY? CLEARLY WOMEN HAVE MADE AND ARE CONTINUING TO MAKE IMPORTANT DISCOVERIES, BUT DO YOU THINK THEIR ACHIEVEMENTS ARE STILL OVERLOOKED?
TIME MACHINE
HOPEFULLY RAISING AN AWARENESS OF WOMEN IN SCIENCE WILL ENCOURAGE GIRLS TO BE THE NEXT GENERATION OF AWESOME SCIENTISTS.
TIME MACHINE
THERE ARE SOME GREAT ORGANISATIONS OUT THERE LIKE STEMNET WHO AIM TO INSPIRE YOUNG PEOPLE (ESPECIALLY GIRLS) TO GET INVOLVED IN SCIENCE, TECHNOLOGY, ENGINEERING AND MATHEMATICS (STEM), AND WISE, WHOSE MISSION IS TO GET 1 MILLION MORE WOMEN INTO THE UK STEM WORKFORCE. THERE ARE MORE ORGANISATIONS ACROSS THE WORLD WORKING TOWARDS THE SAME GOAL, TOO. LET'S HOPE THAT THEY WILL HELP TO MAKE A DIFFERENCE.
THAT'S KAYLA LACOVINO. NOT ONLY IS SHE A PIONEERING FEMALE VOLCANOLOGIST, BUT SHE USES SOCIAL MEDIA TO REALLY HELP MAKE HER WORK REACHABLE TO AS MANY GROUPS AS POSSIBLE.
THERE'S PEGGY WHITSON! SHE WAS THE FIRST FEMALE COMMANDER OF THE INTERNATIONAL SPACE STATION!
WHAT DO YOU THINK SHE SEES ON OUR BRAIN SCANS?
I DUNNO, BUT I BET THEY PROVE WE ARE SUPER SMART!
ALL THIS TIME TRAVELLING IS EXHAUSTING!
MIGHTY WOMEN OF SCIENCE
YEAH BUT I THINK WE HAVE ENOUGH SCIENTISTS TO MAKE OUR BOOK, WE ARE NEARLY FINISHED!
LOOK AT ALL THE MIGHTY WOMEN WE'VE VISITED, THEY'VE DONE SO MUCH FOR THE WORLD.
I'M SO GLAD WE WERE ABLE TO SHARE THEIR STORIES.
WHAT DO YOU THINK IS NEXT FOR OUR MIGHTY WOMEN OF SCIENCE?
WANNA FIND OUT...?
TIME MACHINE

"I want to make sure we use all our talent, not just 25 percent. Don't let anyone rob you of your imagination, your creativity, or your curiosity. It's your place in the world; it's your life. Go on and do all you can with it, and make it the life you want to live."

Mae Jemison: the first African American woman in space

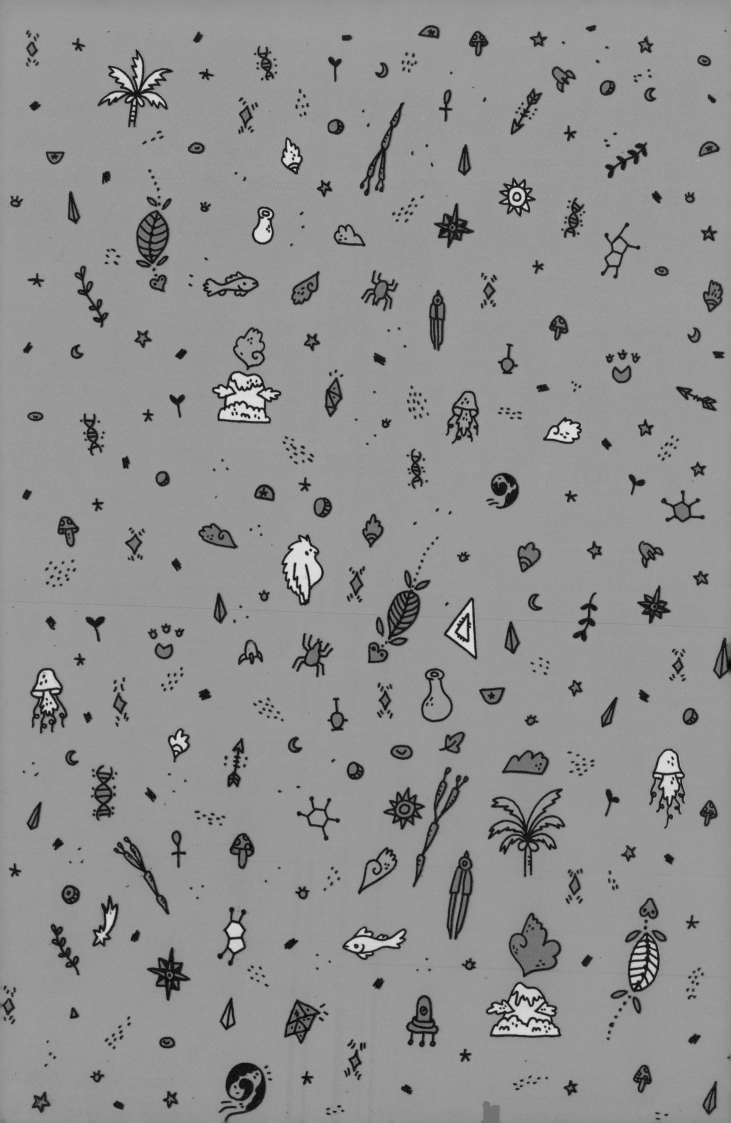